BABY AFGHANS
to knit and crochet

Leisure Arts, Inc. • Maumelle Arkansas

INTRODUCTION

We know that you probably dislike making gauge swatches; and you may think that since an afghan doesn't have to fit anyone, if your gauge is a bit off, it won't matter. But it really will matter: if you're working too tightly, you'll get a smaller afghan than planned; and if too loosely, you may wind up with not enough yarn to complete the project. So, please — take the few extra minutes needed to work up a 4" gauge swatch, in the pattern stitch specified, before you start any afghan. Change needle or hook size as needed to achieve the correct gauge.If you have any difficulty understanding the instructions, or find any errors in any of the patterns, please write to us and we will make every effort to assist you. We would also enjoy hearing your comments on this leaflet, and suggestions for other patterns you'd like to have us publish.

Janet Rondeau
Design Director

SPECIAL ABBREVIATIONS
CO — cast on
BO — bind off
patt — pattern

BASIC FRINGE INSTRUCTIONS

Cut a piece of cardboard about 6" wide and half as long as specified in instructions for finished strands. Wind yarn loosely around cardboard, cut across one end when card is filled. Cut a big pile of strands and then start fringing; you can wind more strands as you need them.

Fringe with wrong side of afghan facing you. Put the number of strands specified for one tassel together and fold in half. With crochet hook ***(Fig. 1)*** draw folded end through space or st, pull loose ends through folded section and draw knot up tightly ***(Fig. 2)***. Repeat, spaced as specified in individual afghan instructions. Trim ends to even off.

FIG. 1

FIG. 2

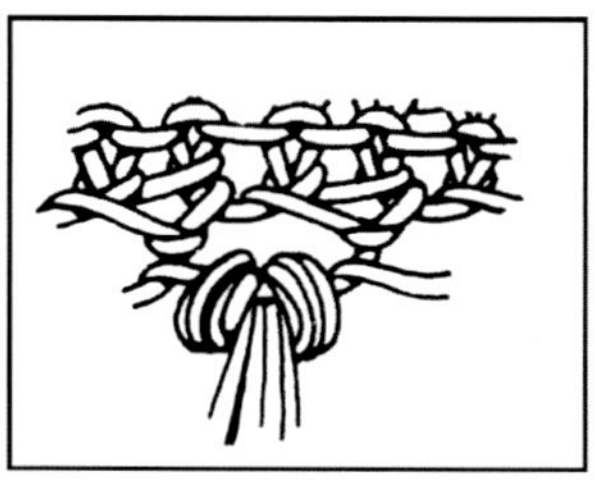

1
BUTTERCUP SQUARES

designed by Jean Leinhauser

Approx finished size: 34" x 45"

Materials: Worsted weight yarn, 20 oz. white, 4 oz. yellow; crochet hook size H (Canadian size 6) or size needed for gauge.

Gauge: 1 square = 5½" square

INSTRUCTIONS

Square (make 48): With yellow, ch 5, join with a sl st to form a ring. **Rnd 1:** Draw up loop on hook to ½", * (YO, insert hook into ring and draw up a loop to measure ½" [see **Fig. 3**]) twice; you should now have 5 loops on hook. YO and draw through first 4 loops, YO and draw through rem 2 loops; you have now completed one cluster. Ch 1. Rep from * 7 times, join with a sl st to top of first cluster (**Fig. 4**).

FIG. 3

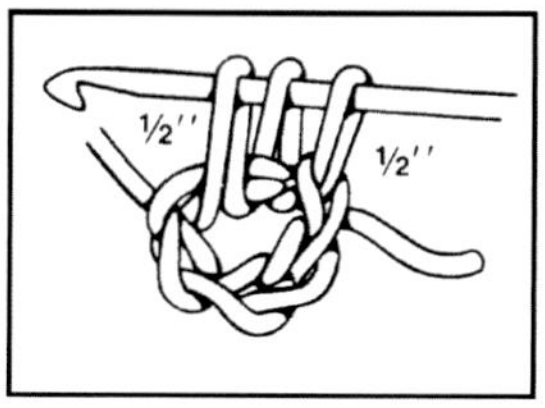

FIG. 4

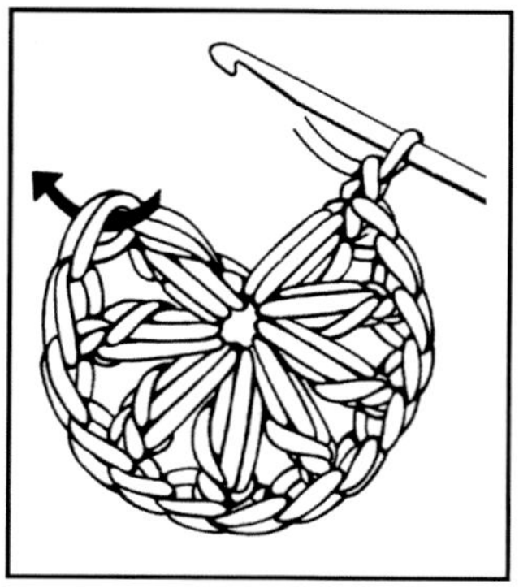

You should now have 8 clusters, each separated by a ch-1 sp. Finish off yellow.

Rnd 2: Join white with a sl st in any ch-1 sp. Draw up loop on hook to ½"; work a cluster, ch 3; in same sp work another cluster (this forms a corner), ch 1, * (cluster, ch 1, cluster) all in next sp; ch 1, (cluster, ch 3, cluster) all in next sp for corner; ch 1. Rep from * twice; (cluster, ch 1, cluster) all in next sp; ch 1, join with a sl st to ch-3 sp of first corner group; you should have 16 clusters.

Rnd 3: Draw up loop on hook to ½", (cluster, ch 3, cluster) all in same sp; ch 1, * (cluster, ch 1, cluster) in next sp; ch 1, cluster in next sp, ch 1, (cluster, ch 1, cluster) in next sp; ch 1, (cluster, ch 3, cluster) in next ch-3 corner sp; ch 1, rep from * twice; (cluster, ch 1, cluster) in next sp; ch 1, cluster in next sp: ch 1, (cluster, ch 1, cluster) in next sp; ch 1, join with a sl st to ch-3 sp of starting corner group; you should have 28 clusters.

Rnd 4: Draw up loop on hook to ½", (cluster, ch 3, cluster) all in same sp; ch 1, * cluster, ch 1, in each of next 6 sps; (cluster, ch 3, cluster) in corner sp; ch 1, rep from * twice; (cluster, ch 1) in each of next 6 sps, join with a sc to ch-3 sp of starting corner group; you should have 32 clusters.

Rnd 5: Work 2 more sc in ch-3 sp, * sc in each cluster and each sp to next corner, 3 sc in ch-3 sp; rep from * twice, sc in each cluster and each sp to end, join with a sl st to starting sc of rnd. Finish off.

Joining: With right sides of two squares facing, join white with a sl st through corner sc of both squares. Carefully matching sts, sc in each sc across one side. Finish off.

Continue joining in this manner, taking care to match stitches, until you have a strip of 8 squares. Make 5 more strips of 8 squares. Join these six strips in same manner; afghan is six squares wide by eight squares long. Lightly steam seams.

Edging

Rnd 1: Join yellow with a sc in any corner sp. Ch 1, sc in same sp; sc in each sc across side; in next corner work (sc, ch 1, sc); continue to work sc around, working rem corners in same manner. Join. Finish off yellow.

Rnd 2: Join white with a sl st in any corner sp; ch 3, hdc in same sp, hdc in each sc to next corner sp; work (hdc, ch 1, hdc) in corner sp; continue to work hdc around, working rem corners in same manner. Join. Finish off white.

Rnd 3: Join yellow with a sc in any corner. Work as for edging Rnd 1, working one sc in each hdc, and (sc, ch 1, sc) in each corner sp. Finish off. Lightly steam edging.

2

GRANNY SQUARE

designed by Jean Leinhauser

Approx size before fringe: 41" x 51"

Materials: Worsted weight yarn, 20 oz. white, 4 oz. yellow, 8 oz. pink, 12 oz. green; crochet hook size H (Canadian size 6), or size needed for gauge.

Gauge: One 3-round square = 3"; one block of 4 squares and two rows of border = 7½".

BASIC GRANNY SQUARE INSTRUCTIONS

With first color, ch 3, join with a sl st to form a ring.

Rnd 1: Ch 3, work 2 dc in ring; ch 1, * 3 dc in ring, ch 1, rep from * twice, join last ch-1 to top of starting ch with a sl st. End off first color.

Rnd 2: With right side of work facing, join second color with a sl st in any ch-1 sp; ch 3, work (2 dc, ch 1, 3 dc) all in same sp; * in next ch-1 sp, work (3 dc, ch 1, 3 dc); rep from * twice. Join with a sl st to top of starting ch of rnd. End off second color.

Rnd 3: With right side facing, join third color with a sl st in any ch-1 sp; (ch 3, 2 dc, ch 1, 3 dc) all in the same sp; * 3 dc in next sp between groups for side. In next corner ch-1 sp, work (3 dc, ch 1, 3 dc) all in same sp; rep from * twice; 3 dc in next side sp, join with a sl st to top of starting ch of rnd. End off third color.

NOTE: When a pattern calls for working 2 or more rnds of the same color in succession, at the end of the first rnd, join by working a sl st in the ch-3 of the preceding rnd, but do not cut yarn. Sl st in tops of next 2 dc, sl st in the corner sp. This brings yarn to the correct position for the start of the next rnd.

Instructions for 4-Square Block (make 30): Following Basic Granny Square Instructions above, work four squares with **Rnd 1,** yellow; **Rnd 2,** pink; **Rnd 3,** green. Sew these four squares tog to make a block, being careful to have right sides facing and to join corners at center neatly.

Border: Join white in any corner sp.

Rnd 1: Ch 3, (2 dc, ch 1, 3 dc) all in same sp; * 3 dc in each sp along side, and in sp between squares, to next corner (3 dc, ch 1, 3 dc) in next corner; rep from * twice, 3 dc in each sp to last corner, join with a sl st; sl st to ch-1 sp of same corner.

Rnd 2: Ch 3, (2 dc, ch 1, 3 dc) in corner sp, continue in patt around. Finish off.

Finishing: Taking care to keep right sides of work facing, sew blocks tog in rows of 5 blocks across and 6 blocks down; join white in any corner sp and work patt for 2 rnds. Finish off.

Fringe: Following Basic Fringe Instructions, cut 12" strands of white. Each tassel is composed of six strands; place one tassel in each sp across short ends of afghan.

3

KNITTED RIPPLE

designed by Meredith Montross

Approx size before fringe: 32" x 41"

Materials: Worsted weight yarn, 12 oz. white, 4 oz. blue, 4 oz. pink; size 9 (Canadian size 4) 14" straight or 29" circular knitting needles; crochet hook size H (Canadian size 6), or size needed for gauge.

Gauge: In patt st: 11 sts = 2¼"
28 rows = 4¼"

To test gauge, CO 33 sts and work 28 patt rows. Your swatch should measure about 6¾" x 4¼".

SPECIAL NOTES

SSK: The abbreviation "SSK" used in this pattern means to work as follows: slip the next two sts **knitwise,** one at a time, then insert the tip of left-hand needle into **fronts** of these two sts from the left, and knit them tog from this position.

Pattern Stitch (multiple of 11):
Odd numbered rows are wrong side rows.

Rows 1-5: Knit.

Row 6: * K2 tog, K2, knit into front and back of each of next 2 sts, K3, SSK; rep from * across.

Rows 7, 9 and 11: Purl.

Rows 8, 10 and 12: * K2 tog, K2, knit into front and back of each of next 2 sts, K3, SSK; rep from * across.

INSTRUCTIONS: With white, CO 154 sts. (Note: it is not necessary, but will be easier for you to keep track of patt sts if you place a marker every 22 sts). * Work Patt Rows 1-5. Drop white (do not break off; you may carry it loosely along the side as you work up afghan). Attach blue and work Rows 6-11. Break off blue and with white work Rows 12 and 1-5. Drop white and with pink work Rows 6-11. Break off pink and with white work Row 12. Rep from * until piece measures about 41", ending with a blue stripe; then work Patt Rows 12 and 1-4 in white. BO.

Finishing: Weave in yarn ends. With crochet hook and white, work one row of sc along both sides of afghan, being sure to catch the white yarn that was loosely carried up sides.

Fringe: Following Basic Fringe Instructions, cut 10" strands of white. Each tassel is composed of seven strands; evenly space 29 tassels across each short end of the afghan.

4
CROCHET RIPPLE
designed by Marion Graham

Approx size before fringe: 30" x 40"

Materials: Worsted weight yarn, 16 oz. pink, 4 oz. white; crochet hook size I (Canadian size 4), or size needed for gauge.

Gauge: 4 dc = 1"
3 rows = 2"

INSTRUCTIONS
Wide Strip (make 3)

Row 1: With pink, ch 23, dc in 4th ch from hook and in each of next 8 chs; 3 dc in next ch (inc made); dc in each of next 10 chs, ch 3, turn. You should have 23 dcs.

Row 2: (YO, insert hook in **back loop** of next dc, hook yarn and draw through; YO and draw through 2 loops) twice, YO and draw through all 3 loops on hook (dec made).

Note: From now on work in **back loop only** of each dc. Dc in each of next 8 dc, 3 dc in next dc (inc made), dc in each of next 8 dc, dec as before over next 2 sts, dc in top of turning ch; ch 3, turn.

Rep Row 2 until piece measures about 40", measuring at center 3-dc point of strip.

Narrow Strip (make 2)
Row 1: With pink, ch 11, dc in 4th ch from hook and in each of next 2 chs; 3 dc in next ch (inc made), dc in each of last 4 chs; ch 3, turn. You should have 11 dcs.

Row 2: Dec over first 2 dc as above, dc in each of next 2 dc, 3 dc in next dc (inc made), dc in each of next 2 dc, dec over next 2 dc, dc in top of turning ch; ch 3, turn.

Rep Row 2 until strip has same number of rows as wide strip. Finish off.

Finishing: With long edge of any strip across top, join pink with sl st in upper right-hand corner.

Row 1: Sc in same sp, work 2 sc in each row across long edge. Finish off.

Row 2: With same side facing, join white with sl st in first sc of prev row. Ch 3, dc in 2nd sc and in each sc across. Finish off.

Making sure that the same side of each strip is facing, rep Rows 1 and 2 across each long edge of each strip. Sew strips tog, alternating one wide with one narrow.

SIDE BORDER:
Row 1: With right side facing and long edge across top, join white with sl st in dc at upper right-hand corner. Ch 3, dc in back loop of 2nd dc and in each dc across.

Rep SIDE BORDER, Row 1 across opposite long edge.

Fringe: Following Basic Fringe Instructions, cut 10" strands of yarn. There are 24 white tassels, with 5 strands each. Place one white tassel in each short end of each white dc row. There are 54 pink tassels, with 5 strands each. Place one pink tassel in every 3rd pink dc across each short end: you should have 7 pink tassels in wide strips and 3 pink tassels in narrow strips.

Cover garments made by Diane Kingwill, Rachel Kyle, Margaret Miller and Kathie Schroeder.

Made in U.S.A.